Low Point
to **No Point**

Over 60 recipes for 6 Points and under

SIMON & SCHUSTER
A VIACOM COMPANY

Joy Skipper

First published in Great Britain by Simon & Schuster UK Ltd, 2003
A Viacom Company

© Weight Watchers International Inc. 2003. All rights reserved.
No part of this publication may be reproduced, stored or
transmitted in any form or by any means without the prior
permission of Weight Watchers (UK) Ltd. Weight Watchers®,
Points® and **Time To Eat**™ are trademarks of Weight Watchers
International Inc. and used under its control by Weight
Watchers (UK) Ltd.

Simon & Schuster UK Ltd
Africa House
64–78 Kingsway
London
WC2B 6AH

This book is copyright under the Berne Convention.
All rights reserved.

Photography and styling by Steve Baxter
Food preparation by Carol Tennant
Design by Jane Humphrey
Typesetting by Stylize Digital Artwork
Printed and bound in Hong Kong

Weight Watchers Publications Manager: Corrina Griffin
Weight Watchers Publications Executives: Lucy Davidson,
Mandy Spittle
Weight Watchers Publications Assistant: Nina Bhogal

A CIP catalogue for this book is available from the British Library

ISBN 0 74323 899 0

Pictured on the front cover: Home Made Pizza, page 26
Pictured on the back cover: Chocolate Orange Brownies, page 23
Pictured on the title page: French Apple Tart, page 33

Raw Eggs: Only the freshest eggs should be used. Pregnant
women, the elderly and children should avoid recipes with
eggs which are not fully cooked or raw.

All fruits, vegetables and eggs are medium size unless otherwise
stated.

Recipe timings are approximate and meant to be guidelines.
Please note that the preparation time includes all the steps
up to and following the main cooking time(s).

 You'll find this easy to read logo on every recipe throughout the book. The logo represents the number of Points per serving each recipe contains. The easy to use Points system is designed to help you eat what you want, when you want – as long as you stay within your Points allowance – giving you the freedom to enjoy the food you love.

This symbol denotes a vegetarian recipe and assumes vegetarian cheese and free range eggs are used. Virtually fat free fromage frais and low fat crème fraîche may contain traces of gelatine so they are not always vegetarian: please check the labels.

This symbol denotes a vegan dish.

contents

delicious
recipes for
6 Points and Under!

Do you ever find yourself at the end of the day, with only a few Points to spare and little inspiration? Do you ever wish you had a few more Points in the day? If so, then this is the cookbook for you! Welcome to Low Point to No Point – the cookbook that makes your Points go further! Over 60 sensational recipes, all for 6 Points and Under! And... to make life even simpler, we have organised the chapters by Points, to allow you to find the perfect meal in a matter of minutes!

This book will teach you how to make delicious and filling meals with the minimum of fuss, will inspire you to create wonderful flavours and tastes for just a few Points and will show you how to get the most out of your food even if you have no Points to spare... Already sound too good to be true? Just keep on reading!

Fancy a three course meal for just 1½ Points? Why not try Spicy Butternut Squash Soup (page 9) followed by Mushroom Stroganoff (page 10) and then finish it off with the delightful Lemon Soufflé (page 13)? Perhaps you're bored of sandwiches for lunch and want something different – well then there's plenty to choose from – try the Lentil and Herb Salad (page 18) or the Turkey and Spinach Samosas (page 6). No matter how many Points you want to spend, with over 60 recipes to choose from, you're sure to find the ideal meal or snack to suit your mood.

Some of the recipes are old favourites that we enjoy again and again, such as Spaghetti Bolognese (page 34) or Queen of Puddings (page 43). Other recipes take advantage of fresh and exotic ingredients that are now available in the supermarkets all year round. Whether it's hot and spicy you're after or something sweet and satisfying – there is something here to suit every occasion.

We all live such busy lives these days, so it's important that cooking at the end of the day is simple – and fun too! That's why these recipes are not only scrumptious and satisfying, but they're quick and easy to make. This book is a wonderful resource, full of Low Point to No Point recipes that you'll be able to savour again and again! Weight Loss has never been easier – with Weight Watchers and Time To Eat.

1 Point
and under

It's hard to imagine substantial and tasty meals for 1 Point or less, but you'll find lots of them here – they're all delicious, healthy and filling too. These recipes are ideal for when you've used up most of your Points but you still want a little something more, or if you want to save up Points for a special treat.

TURKEY AND SPINACH SAMOSAS

17½ Points per recipe
Makes 15
Preparation time: 35 minutes
Cooking time: 15 minutes
Calories per serving: 75
Freezing: recommended for up to 1 month

These are great to take on a picnic or in your lunchbox to the office. If you love really spicy food then just increase the chilli powder to your liking. Try serving these samosas with a No Point crisp green salad.

low fat cooking spray

1 small onion, diced finely

1 garlic clove, crushed

280 g (9¾ oz) turkey mince

1 teaspoon ground cumin

1 teaspoon ground coriander

1 teaspoon chilli powder

½ teaspoon ground ginger

175 g (6 oz) frozen chopped spinach, defrosted and drained

15 sheets of 28½ cm × 43½ cm filo pastry

salt and freshly ground black pepper

1 Preheat the oven to Gas Mark 6/ 200°C/fan oven 180°C.

2 Spray a medium saucepan with low fat cooking spray. Add the onion, garlic and turkey mince and cook for 5–6 minutes, stirring occasionally to brown the meat.

3 Add the spices and stir well before adding the spinach and seasoning. Mix together and heat to a gentle simmer. Simmer for 15 minutes.

4 Leave the mixture to cool slightly. Lay the filo pastry on the work surface. Lay one sheet on a chopping board large enough for the whole sheet. Spray the pastry with low fat cooking spray and then lay another sheet on top. Repeat this until you have three sheets of filo on top of each other.

5 Cut the stack of filo sheets lengthways into 3.

6 Place a heaped tablespoon of the turkey and spinach mixture at the bottom of each strip of pastry. To fold into a samosa shape, lift one of the corners at the bottom of the pastry strip (nearest the filling) and bring it diagonally over the filling to the other side. This will give you a triangle shape. Pick up the point of the triangle and fold the filled pastry over diagonally. Keep folding over and over until you reach the top of the pastry strip and have a triangular samosa.

7 Repeat the process with the remaining pastry and turkey mixture to make 15 samosas.

8 Place the samosas on a baking sheet and spray them with low fat cooking spray.

9 Bake the samosas in the oven for 15 minutes until golden.

Top tip Cover the filo sheets you are not working on with a damp cloth to prevent them from drying out.

Variation The turkey mince can be substituted for extra lean minced beef, minced lamb or chicken if wished. If you use beef or lamb each samosa will be 1½ Points; if you use chicken mince, then each samosa will be 1 Point.

Turkey and Spinach
Samosas: Enjoy a
spicy samosa for
only 1 Point.

Pesto Roast
Peppers: Two
delicious pepper
halves for just
1 Point.

PESTO ROAST PEPPERS

3 Points per recipe

Ⓥ Serves 4

Preparation time: 15 minutes

Cooking time: 45–50 minutes

Calories per serving: 110

Freezing: not recommended

These roast peppers, served with a No Point crunchy salad, make a wonderful lunchtime snack. They are delicious eaten hot or cold.

4 red peppers, de-seeded and halved

3 spring onions, sliced

1 courgette, sliced

1 carrot, diced

2 tomatoes, diced

1 garlic clove, sliced

30 g (1¼ oz) pesto

salt and freshly ground black pepper

fresh basil leaves, torn, to garnish

1 Preheat the oven to Gas Mark 6/ 200°C/fan oven 180°C.

2 Place the pepper halves in a roasting tin, skin side down.

3 Place the remaining ingredients in a bowl and mix well to coat everything with the pesto.

4 Spoon the vegetable mixture into the peppers and bake for 45–50 minutes until the vegetables are soft.

5 Garnish with the chopped basil. Serve two roasted pepper halves per person.

Variation Try topping the peppers, after 20 minutes of cooking, with 50 g (1¾ oz) of grated mozzarella light cheese and then returning them to the oven for the remaining 25–30 minutes. The Points will be 1½ per serving.

TOMATO AND BASIL SOUP

1½ Points per recipe

Ⓥ Ⓥⓖ Serves 4

Preparation time: 15 minutes

Cooking time: 30 minutes

Calories per serving: 70

Freezing: recommended

This refreshing and summery soup, served with plenty of freshly chopped basil, is delicious served either hot or cold.

1 kg (2 lb 4 oz) ripe tomatoes, halved

3 shallots, peeled and halved

1 garlic clove, sliced

2 teaspoons olive oil

12 fresh basil leaves

salt and freshly ground black pepper

1 Preheat the oven to Gas Mark 6/ 200°C/fan oven 180°C.

2 Place the tomatoes, shallots and garlic in a roasting tin.

3 Pour over the olive oil. Season well and toss everything to coat them with the oil.

4 Roast for 30 minutes.

5 Put the roasted ingredients into a food processor or blender, along with half of the basil leaves. Blend until nearly smooth. Reheat in a pan for 5 or 6 minutes.

6 Shred the remaining basil leaves and stir them into the soup.

7 Ladle the soup into four bowls and serve.

Top tip If you want a really smooth soup, sieve it after blending.

Variation If serving this soup cold, add some crushed ice cubes and top with a few torn basil leaves.

SPICY BUTTERNUT SQUASH SOUP

0 Points per recipe

Ⓥ Ⓥⓖ Serves: 4

Preparation and cooking time: 35 minutes

Calories per serving: 50

Freezing: recommended for up to 1 month

low fat cooking spray

1 onion, chopped

400 g (14 oz) butternut squash, peeled, de-seeded and chopped

2 teaspoons ground cumin

850 ml (1½ pints) vegetable stock

salt and freshly ground black pepper

1 Spray a medium saucepan with low fat cooking spray. Add the onion and sauté for 3–4 minutes until it begins to soften.

2 Add the butternut squash and cumin and stir well.

3 Pour in the stock and bring to the boil. Simmer for 18–20 minutes until the butternut squash is tender.

4 Remove from the heat and blend in a food processor or with a hand blender.

5 Check the seasoning and serve.

MUSHROOM STROGANOFF

3 Points per recipe

Ⓥ *Serves 4*

Preparation time: 10 minutes

Cooking time: 25 minutes

Calories per serving: 65

*Freezing: recommended for up to
1 month*

This creamy, filling stroganoff can
be made hotter if you wish just by
adding slightly more paprika. Serve
this dish with freshly cooked runner
beans for no extra Points.

low fat cooking spray
1 large onion, chopped
450 g (1 lb) chestnut mushrooms, quartered
2 teaspoons paprika
400 g (14 oz) canned chopped tomatoes
2 tablespoons half fat crème fraîche
salt and freshly ground black pepper

1 Spray a medium saucepan with
low fat cooking spray and add the
onion. Cover and leave to sweat on
a low heat for 4–6 minutes, until
the onion starts to soften.

2 Add the mushrooms and stir in the
paprika. Cook for 1–2 minutes.

3 Pour in the tomatoes with 150 ml
(5 fl oz) water. Bring the mixture to
a simmer and continue to simmer for
15 minutes.

4 Remove the pan from the heat and
stir in the crème fraîche. Check and
add seasoning to taste. Serve on four
warmed plates.

Variations Shiitake or oyster mushrooms
also work well in this recipe.

Try serving this dish with 4
tablespoons of cooked rice to soak
up all the lovely sauce. This will
add an extra 3 Points per serving.

**Grapefruit and
Beetroot Salad:
A sensational
starter for only
½ a Point.**

GRAPEFRUIT AND BEETROOT SALAD

1 Point per recipe

Ⓥ Ⓥ͛ *Serves 2*

Preparation time: 10 minutes

Calories per serving: 100

Freezing: not recommended

This salad is lovely and refreshing
when served on a warm summer's
day.

1 grapefruit, segmented
25 g (1 oz) watercress
25 g (1 oz) baby spinach leaves
185 g (6½ oz) fresh beetroot, cooked
1 teaspoon tahini
salt and freshly ground black pepper

1 Mix the grapefruit and vegetables
together in a salad bowl.

2 Mix the tahini with 1 tablespoon
of water and pour this into the
salad bowl.

3 Toss gently to coat all the
ingredients with the tahini dressing,
season and serve.

Variation For a main meal salad,
add 100 g (3½ oz) cooked chicken,
or 100 g (3½ oz) canned butter
beans for a vegetarian version. The
Points will be 1½ and 1 per serving
respectively.

SQUID SALAD

4 Points per recipe

Serves 4

Preparation and cooking time:
20 minutes

Calories per serving: 125

Freezing: not recommended

A deliciously fresh tasting salad.

For the salad

850 ml (1¹/₂ pints) fish stock

300 g (10¹/₂ oz) fresh squid, sliced,
keeping the tentacles whole

1 cucumber, de-seeded, cut in half
lengthways, then sliced thinly into
half moons

1 tablespoon sesame seeds

100 g (3¹/₂ oz) Chinese leaves, chopped

For the dressing

juice of 1 lime

1 teaspoon fish sauce

1 tablespoon soy sauce

1 fresh red chilli, de-seeded and
chopped finely

2 spring onions, sliced

1 teaspoon caster sugar

2 tablespoons chopped fresh coriander

salt and freshly ground black pepper

1 Whisk all the dressing ingredients together except for the fresh coriander.

2 In a medium saucepan bring the stock to a gentle simmer and add the squid. Simmer for 3–4 minutes.

3 Drain the squid and put it into a bowl.

4 Add the freshly chopped coriander to the dressing and then pour it over the squid. Leave to cool slightly.

5 Add the cucumber slices, sesame seeds and Chinese leaves to the bowl and mix gently.

6 Check the seasoning, adding more if necessary and serve.

COD WITH SALSA

2¹/₂ Points per recipe

Serves 2

Preparation time: 10 minutes

Cooking time: 15-20 minutes

Calories per serving: 110

Freezing: not recommended

This makes a very simple but tasty light lunch.

low fat cooking spray

2 × 90 g (3¹/₄ oz) cod steaks

¹/₂ teaspoon cumin seeds

salt and freshly ground black pepper

For the salsa

3 tomatoes, diced

¹/₂ small red onion, diced

2 tablespoons fresh coriander, chopped

¹/₄ teaspoon ground cumin

juice of ¹/₂ lime

1 Preheat the oven to Gas Mark 4/ 180°C/fan oven 160°C.

2 Spray a shallow ovenproof dish with low fat cooking spray. Place the cod steaks in the dish and season them. Sprinkle with cumin seeds and then spray the steaks with low fat cooking spray. Roast for 15–20 minutes.

3 Meanwhile mix the salsa ingredients together, season and then cover and set aside.

4 Serve the cooked fish with the salsa.

Cod with Salsa: Fantastic fish for just 1 Point.

1 Preheat the oven to Gas Mark 6/ 200°C/fan oven 180°C.

2 Mix together the cumin seeds and all the vegetables, except the spinach, in a large bowl.

3 Pour the mixed vegetables into a roasting tin and spray them with low fat cooking spray.

4 Season well and then place them in the oven for 25 minutes.

5 Toss the vegetables gently and then cook for another 25 minutes.

6 When cooked, remove the vegetables from the oven and spoon them into a large bowl.

7 Lightly toss the vegetables with the baby spinach leaves. The spinach leaves will start to wilt slightly.

8 Sprinkle with the balsamic vinegar and serve.

Variation Most vegetables can be cooked in this way, just choose your No Point favourites and mix and match!

No Point Roast Veggies: Wow – No Points at all!

NO POINT ROAST VEGGIES

0 Points per recipe

Ⓥ Ⓥⓖ *Serves 4*

Preparation time: 20 minutes

Cooking time: 50 minutes

Calories per serving: 100

Freezing: not recommended

This dish is so easy, yet so delicious. All the vegetables are No Points so you can serve it with any of your favourite meat or fish recipes.

2 teaspoons cumin seeds

½ butternut squash, peeled, de-seeded and chopped into bite size pieces

1 leek, sliced into bite size pieces

1 courgette, sliced into bite size pieces

1 red onion, chopped into bite size pieces

1 red pepper, de-seeded and chopped into bite size pieces

1 yellow pepper, de-seeded and chopped into bite size pieces

2 celery sticks, sliced into bite size pieces

low fat cooking spray

185 g (6½ oz) baby spinach leaves

2 tablespoons balsamic vinegar

salt and freshly ground black pepper

LEMON SOUFFLES

3½ Points per recipe

 Serves 4

Preparation and cooking time:
30 minutes
Calories per serving: 55
Freezing: not recommended

Soufflés are ideal for when you are entertaining as they always look so impressive – and no one will guess how low these are in Points!

low fat cooking spray
2 teaspoons caster sugar
grated zest of 1 lemon
3 tablespoons lemon curd
3 large egg whites

1 Preheat the oven to Gas Mark 6/200°C/fan oven 180°C.

2 Spray four medium ramekin dishes with low fat cooking spray. Using 1 teaspoon of caster sugar, coat the dishes by shaking the sugar around one dish and then sprinkling the excess into the next one. Do this until the teaspoon of sugar is used.

3 In a small bowl, beat the lemon zest into the lemon curd.

4 In a large grease free bowl, whisk the egg whites until stiff. Add the remaining caster sugar and whisk for 1 minute more.

5 Fold the lemon curd mixture into the egg whites.

6 Spoon the soufflé mixture into the four ramekin dishes. Place them on a baking tray and cook in the oven for 10–12 minutes until the soufflés are risen and golden. Serve immediately.

Top tip Always make sure the bowl you are using to whisk egg whites is completely free of grease, or the egg whites will not whisk up.

Variations This recipe also works well with orange curd and orange zest. The Points will remain the same.

If you want to make the soufflés a little richer, place an additional half teaspoon of lemon curd in the bottom of the ramekin dish before adding the egg white mixture. The Points will remain the same.

ETON MESS

2½ Points per recipe

 Serves 2

Preparation time: 5 minutes
Calories per serving: 75
Freezing: not recommended

A fantastically, simple recipe – sweet and satisfying and just 1 Point!

1 meringue nest
100 ml (3½ fl oz) very low fat plain yogurt
150 g (5½ oz) fresh strawberries, sliced or chopped
2 passion fruits

1 Break up the meringue nest in a medium bowl.

2 Add the yogurt and strawberries and mix very gently.

3 Divide the mixture between two glasses.

4 Cut the passion fruit in half and scrape out the flesh. Strain the flesh through a sieve and pour the juice over the glasses of Eton Mess. Serve immediately.

Variation Most fruits can be used for this recipe although summer fruits tend to work best. Try using 125 g (4½ oz) raspberries instead of the strawberries. The Points will remain the same. If you want to make a creamier version, try using 0% fat Greek yogurt instead. The Points will remain the same.

Eton Mess: A dreamy dessert for only 1 Point.

2 Points
and under

In this chapter you'll be amazed at the deliciously satisfying snacks, meals and desserts you can enjoy for only 1$\frac{1}{2}$–2 Points. Soups, kebabs, casseroles and even chocolate orange brownies! So, there really is no need for boring diets – get cooking and tuck in to some fantastic food!

STUFFED MUSHROOMS

6 Points per recipe

Ⓥ *Serves 4*

Preparation time: 20 minutes

Cooking time: 40 minutes

Calories per serving: 100

Freezing: not recommended

The colourful layers in these mushrooms look great – and taste fantastic too! Serve these stuffed mushrooms with a No Point salad or green vegetables.

1 butternut squash, peeled, de-seeded and diced
1 courgette, sliced thinly
4 large Portabello mushrooms
2 tomatoes, sliced thinly
100 g (3½ oz) half fat Cheddar cheese, grated
salt and freshly ground black pepper

1 Preheat the oven to Gas Mark 6/ 200°C/fan oven 180°C.

2 Bring a medium saucepan of water to the boil and add the butternut squash. Cook for 8–10 minutes, or until soft. Drain and mash the squash with a potato masher, season well and set aside.

3 Place the mushrooms cup side up in a baking dish or on a baking sheet. Divide the slices of courgette between the four mushrooms, laying them around the stalk, each piece slightly overlapping.

4 Top with slices of tomato in the same way.

5 Place the mashed butternut squash over the tomatoes, forking it around the top, and then sprinkle on the grated cheese.

6 Cook the mushrooms in the oven for 40 minutes.

7 Preheat the grill just before the mushrooms have finished cooking.

8 Place the mushrooms under the grill for another 4–5 minutes for a crisp, cheesy topping.

Stuffed
Mushrooms:
Marvellous
mushrooms
for 1½ Points.

Prawn Noodle Soup: Savour the flavours of the Orient for only 2 Points.

PRAWN NOODLE SOUP

8 Points per recipe

Serves 4

Preparation and cooking time:
25 minutes

Calories per serving: 175

Freezing: not recommended

This Oriental soup has a deliciously
delicate and tasty flavour.

90 g (3¼ oz) egg noodles, broken roughly
1 teaspoon olive oil
2 garlic cloves, crushed
1 cm (½ inch) fresh ginger, peeled and chopped finely
4 spring onions, sliced finely
240 g (8½ oz) fresh, raw king prawns
1.2 litres (2 pints) hot vegetable stock
1 small leek, sliced thinly
salt and freshly ground black pepper

1 Bring a medium saucepan of water
to the boil and add the noodles.
Simmer for 4 minutes. Drain the
noodles and set them aside.

2 Heat the oil in a medium
saucepan. Add the garlic, ginger
and spring onions and stir fry for
2–3 minutes.

3 Add the prawns and stir fry for a
further 1–2 minutes before adding
the stock. Simmer for 2 minutes.

4 Add the noodles and leek to the
pan and cook for a further 2–3
minutes.

5 Check the seasoning and serve in
four warmed bowls.

Variation The prawns can be
substituted for strips of lean pork –
just stir-fry the pork for slightly
longer before adding the stock. The
Points will increase to 2½ per serving.

CARROT AND ORANGE SOUP

5½ Points per recipe

Ⓥ Ⓥᵍ *Serves 4*

Preparation time: 25 minutes

Cooking time: 15–20 minutes

Calories per serving: 160

Freezing: recommended

The combination of fresh carrots and
tangy orange juice makes this
a really refreshing soup.

1 teaspoon olive oil
1 large onion, chopped
700 g (1 lb 9 oz) carrots, grated
300 g (10½ oz) potatoes, peeled and grated
grated zest and juice of 1 orange
600 ml (1 pint) boiling water
salt and freshly ground black pepper

To garnish

1 orange, segmented
1 tablespoon chopped fresh parsley or coriander

1 Heat the oil in a large saucepan.
Stir fry the onion for 3–4 minutes
before adding the carrots, potatoes
and seasoning.

2 Stir the vegetables thoroughly and
then cover the pan. Leave on a low
heat for 5 minutes to allow the
vegetables to sweat.

3 Add the orange zest and then cover
the vegetables with the boiling water.

4 Cover the pan again and simmer
for 15–20 minutes, until the
vegetables are soft.

5 Add the orange juice and purée
the soup in a blender or food
processor.

6 Check the seasoning and serve
garnished with the orange segments
and freshly chopped parsley or
coriander.

Variation For a carrot and coriander
soup, omit the orange rind and
juice and add a small handful of
fresh coriander before covering
and simmering the soup. Use 2
tablespoons of chopped coriander
instead of the segmented orange as
a garnish. The Points per serving will
then be 1.

**Carrot and
Orange Soup:
Each warming
bowlful is only
1½ Points.**

PORK KEBABS

8 Points per recipe

Serves 4

Preparation time: 25 minutes + marinating

Cooking time: 20 minutes

Calories per serving: 215

Freezing: not recommended

These kebabs are great for lunch and especially good if cooked on the barbecue.

4 tablespoons soy sauce

1 garlic clove, crushed

1 teaspoon honey

¹/₂ teaspoon Dijon mustard

300 g (10¹/₂ oz) lean pork, cut into bite size pieces

100 g (3¹/₂ oz) chestnut or button mushrooms, halved

1 red pepper, de-seeded and cut into chunks

1 red onion, cut into chunks

4 cm (1¹/₂ inch) fresh ginger

4 carrots

2 apples, peeled

4 celery sticks

1 In a shallow bowl, mix together the soy sauce, garlic, honey and mustard.

2 Add the pork and stir to coat it with the marinade. Leave, covered, in the fridge for 30 minutes–1 hour.

3 Thread the pork, mushrooms, pepper and onion alternately on to eight small kebab sticks.

4 Heat the grill until it is very hot.

5 Brush the kebabs with any remaining marinade and cook under the grill for 16–18 minutes, turning often and basting with the marinade to retain the moistness and flavour.

6 If you have a food processor, grate the ginger, carrots, apples and celery all together. If not, then grate each by hand and mix them in a large bowl. Divide the mixture between four plates.

7 Serve two kebabs per person on the grated salad.

Top tip These kebabs can also be barbecued – but if you use wooden skewers do remember to soak them in water first to prevent them from burning.

Variations Lean chunks of lamb leg or beef sirloin work just as well in this recipe. The Points will remain the same.

LENTIL AND HERB SALAD

5 Points per recipe

Ⓥ Ⓥⓔ *Serves 4*

Preparation time: 15 minutes

Cooking time: 25 minutes

Calories per serving: 115

Freezing: not recommended

A healthy but also a very filling and tasty salad – eat it on its own or with your favourite fish dish.

100 g (3¹/₂ oz) Puy lentils

1 teaspoon olive oil

1 large red onion, diced

1 garlic clove, sliced

1 courgette, sliced thinly

1 tablespoon balsamic vinegar

a large bunch of fresh mint, chopped

100 g (3¹/₂ oz) baby spinach

salt and freshly ground black pepper

1 Place the lentils in a medium saucepan with about 200 ml (7 fl oz) of water and bring to the boil. Simmer for 15 minutes until the lentils are cooked but still firm. Keep checking that the water doesn't boil dry, and add a little more if necessary.

2 Meanwhile heat the olive oil in a frying pan and add the red onion and garlic. Cook gently, stirring occasionally, until they start to soften.

3 Add the courgette and continue to cook, stirring occasionally, for 6–8 minutes.

4 When the lentils are cooked, add them to the pan with the balsamic vinegar. Stir well and season with salt and freshly ground black pepper. Remove the pan from the heat and add the freshly chopped mint leaves. Leave the mixture to cool slightly.

5 Place the baby spinach in a shallow serving dish or platter and spoon the lentil mixture over the top to serve.

Variation For a spicy, meaty version add 100 g (3¹/₂ oz) chorizo sausage. Chop and add in step two while frying the red onion and garlic. The Points per serving will be 3.

**Pork Kebabs:
Two tasty
kebabs for
2 Points.**

HERB CRUSTED COD

4½ Points per recipe

Serves 2

Preparation time: 25 minutes

Cooking time: 10 minutes

Calories per serving: 115

Freezing: recommended up to 1 month

This is a delicious way to cook fish as the crispy herb topping seals in the flavour. Serve this dish with some No Point vegetables such as cooked carrots and broccoli.

1 teaspoon unsalted butter

½ small onion, chopped finely

½ tablespoon chopped fresh dill

½ tablespoon chopped fresh parsley

3 tablespoons fresh breadcrumbs

2 × 90 g (3¼ oz) medium cod fillets

low fat cooking spray

salt and freshly ground black pepper

1 Preheat the oven to Gas Mark 6/ 200°C/fan oven 180°C.

2 Melt the butter in a small frying pan. Add the onion and sauté for 4–5 minutes until softened. Remove the pan from the heat and leave to cool slightly.

3 Add the herbs, breadcrumbs and seasoning and mix well.

4 Using your hands, squeeze the mixture together to form a kind of paste.

5 Divide the mixture in half and press each half on to the cod fillets.

6 Spray an ovenproof dish with low fat cooking spray. Place the fillets in the dish.

7 Bake in the oven for 10–12 minutes until the topping is golden and the fish is cooked.

Variation Try using different fish such as haddock fillets or even tuna steaks. The Points per serving will then be 2 and 2½ respectively.

SAUSAGE CASSEROLE

9 Points per recipe

Serves 4

Preparation time: 20 minutes

Cooking time: 45 minutes

Calories per serving: 210

Freezing: not recommended

A comforting and filling casserole that is perfect for all the family.

low fat cooking spray

1 large onion, chopped

275 g (9½ oz) low fat sausages, halved

1 red pepper, de-seeded and sliced

1 Savoy cabbage, shredded

400 g can of chopped tomatoes

1½ teaspoons caraway seeds

salt and freshly ground black pepper

1 Preheat the oven to Gas Mark 4/ 180°C/fan oven 160°C.

2 Spray a flameproof casserole dish with low fat cooking spray and cook the onion over a medium heat for 3–4 minutes.

3 Add the sausages, turning them occasionally until they are brown all over.

4 Add the pepper, cabbage, tomatoes, caraway seeds, 4 tablespoons of water and seasoning. Mix well.

5 Bring it all to a gentle simmer, and then cover the dish and transfer to the oven.

6 Cook for 30 minutes and then remove from the oven and stir. Return to the oven and cook for another 15 minutes. Serve hot.

AMARETTI PEACHES

2½ Points per recipe

Ⓥ Serves 2

Preparation and cooking time:
20 minutes

Calories per serving: 195

Freezing: not recommended

Amaretti biscuits with peaches are a real Italian treat. If you can spare the Points, top the peaches with a tablespoon of low fat plain yogurt, adding an extra ½ Point per serving.

2 ripe peaches

3 amaretti biscuits

1 egg white

1 tablespoon reduced sugar apricot jam

1 Preheat the oven to Gas Mark 4/ 180°C/ fan oven 160°C.

2 Cut the peaches in half and take out the stone. Lay them cut side up on a baking tray.

3 Crush the amaretti biscuits just with your hands.

4 In a grease free bowl, whisk the egg white until stiff.

5 Fold the amaretti biscuits and jam into the egg white then divide this mixture between the four peach halves.

6 Cook in the oven for 8–10 minutes, until the tops are golden.

Variation Try using six plums or apricots for this dish. The Points will remain the same.

Amaretti Peaches: An Italian treat for only 1½ Points.

CRUNCHY FRUIT CRUMBLES

5 Points per recipe

Ⓥ ⓋⒼ Serves 4

Preparation and cooking time:
25 minutes

Calories per serving: 80

Freezing: not recommended

Everybody loves a fruit crumble. These are made individually, preventing you from going back for a second helping!

200 g (7 oz) canned pear halves in fruit juice

60 g (2 oz) fresh raspberries

1 teaspoon treacle

2 teaspoons boiling water

60 g (2 oz) no added sugar muesli

1 Preheat the oven to Gas Mark 4/ 180°C/fan oven 160°C.

2 Drain the pears, reserving the juice, and dice the fruit. Divide the pear and raspberries between four ramekin dishes. Drizzle 1 tablespoon of the reserved juice over the top and discard the remaining juice.

3 Place the treacle in a small measuring jug and pour over the boiling water. Stir them together.

4 Place the muesli in a bowl, pour over the treacle liquid and mix together well until all the muesli is coated.

5 Divide the muesli between the four ramekin dishes and place on top of the fruit. Place the dishes on a baking tray.

6 Cook in the oven for 10–12 minutes, until the crumbles are golden and bubbling.

7 Serve the crumbles warm or cold.

Variation 200 g (7 oz) canned mandarins with 60 g (2 oz) fresh peaches are delicious in this recipe. The Points will remain the same.

Chocolate Orange Brownies: Heavenly brownies for only 1½ Points.

CHOCOLATE ORANGE BROWNIES

14½ Points per recipe

Ⓥ Makes 9

Preparation time: 15 minutes

Cooking time: 20 minutes

Calories per serving: 105

Freezing: recommended up to 1 month

Chocolate and orange are two ingredients that were just made for each other, and they taste wonderful in these delicious brownies.

low fat cooking spray

100 g (3½ oz) self raising white flour

4 tablespoons cocoa powder

½ teaspoon baking powder

¼ teaspoon salt

2 egg whites

75 g (2¾ oz) light muscovado sugar

2 eggs, beaten

grated zest of 1 orange

1 Preheat the oven to Gas Mark 5/ 190°C/fan oven 170°C. Spray an 18 cm (7 inch) square tin with low fat cooking spray.

2 Sieve all the dry ingredients together into a bowl.

3 In a grease free bowl whisk the egg whites until they are stiff. Gradually add the sugar and whisk until the mixture is stiff and glossy.

4 Beat the whole eggs and orange zest into the dry ingredients and, 1 tablespoon at a time, start gently folding in the egg white mixture.

5 Spoon the mixture into the prepared tin and bake in the oven for 16–18 minutes.

6 Leave the brownies to cool in the tin, and then turn out and cut them into nine squares.

OATY FRUIT BISCUITS

13 Points per recipe

Ⓥ Ⓥⓔ Makes 6

Preparation time: 20 minutes

Cooking time: 20 minutes

Calories per serving: 150

Freezing: not recommended

A little like flapjack, these biscuits are perfect for a mid morning snack.

120 g (4¼ oz) dried pears, chopped

grated rind of 1 lemon

6 tablespoons orange juice

150 g (5½ oz) rolled oats

low fat cooking spray

1 Preheat the oven to Gas Mark 6/ 200°C/fan oven 180°C.

2 Place the pears in a small pan with the lemon rind and orange juice.

Bring to a gentle simmer and simmer for 8–10 minutes until the pears are softened and have absorbed half of the juice.

3 Purée the pears and juice in a blender.

4 Mix the purée with the oats. Spray a 20 cm (8 inch) loose bottomed tin with low fat cooking spray and press the mixture into the bottom of the tin.

5 Cook in the oven for 18–20 minutes until golden.

6 Remove from the oven and cut into six wedges. Leave to cool in the tin.

Variations Most dried fruits work in this recipe: try apricots or prunes which make it a bit stickier. The Points will be 1½ and 2 respectively.

Oaty Fruit Biscuits: The perfect snack for 2 Points.

3 Points
and under

Here are more of your favourite recipes with lots of new and exciting ones too – all for only 2¹/₂–3 Points per serving. Some of the recipes can be made in minutes, to be shared with friends, such as Primavera Pasta (page 30). Others will make your mouth water, like Spicy Banana Muffins (page 31) or Rhubarb Fool (page 33) so go on, indulge yourself – but without the guilt!

TERIYAKI CHICKEN SALAD

9¹/₂ Points per recipe
Serves 4
Preparation and cooking time:
25 minutes + 30 minutes marinating
Calories per serving: 185
Freezing: not recommended

This tangy salad is an ideal starter for a dinner party – it will certainly wake up your tastebuds!

| 1 teaspoon groundnut oil |
| 3 tablespoons soy sauce |
| 1 garlic clove, crushed |
| 2 tablespoons sherry |
| grated zest and segments of 1 orange |
| 4 spring onions, sliced |
| 3 × 165 g (5³/₄ oz) skinless chicken breasts, cut into strips |
| 100 g (3¹/₂ oz) pak choi |
| 50 g (1³/₄ oz) fresh beansprouts |

1 Mix together the groundnut oil, soy sauce, garlic, sherry, orange zest and the spring onions.
2 Place the chicken in this marinade. Cover with clingfilm and place in the fridge for 30 minutes.
3 Heat a griddle or wok and with a slotted spoon, transfer the chicken pieces to it. Reserve the marinade.

4 Cook for 6–8 minutes, turning often, until the chicken is cooked through. Pour over the remaining marinade and cook for 1 or 2 minutes.
5 Divide the pak choi, orange segments and beansprouts between four plates or shallow bowls and pour over the chicken pieces and juices. Serve.

Top tip Always make sure you heat the griddle or wok to a good temperature before you start cooking.

Variation For a more substantial meal, cook 60 g (2 oz) of egg noodles to serve with this dish. This will add an extra 3 Points per serving.

Teriyaki Chicken Salad: Enjoy this fabulous Oriental salad for 2½ Points.

**Cullen Skink:
Just 3 Points for
this wonderful
winter warmer!**

CULLEN SKINK

13 Points per recipe

Serves 4

Preparation time: 15 minutes

Cooking time: 15–20 minutes

Calories per serving: 235

Freezing: not recommended

This traditional Scottish soup is named after a small fishing port in Scotland.

400 g (14 oz) smoked haddock fillets

1 bay leaf

400 ml (14 fl oz) semi skimmed milk

1 teaspoon unsalted butter

1 large onion, chopped

3 × 150 g (5½ oz) potatoes, peeled and diced

salt and freshly ground black pepper

freshly chopped chives or parsley, to serve

1 Place the haddock fillets and bay leaf in a medium saucepan and cover with the milk. Simmer for 6–8 minutes, and then drain and reserve the milk and fish. Flake the fish into bite size pieces.

2 Melt the butter in a medium saucepan and sauté the onion for 3–4 minutes.

3 Add the potatoes and stir before adding the reserved milk.

4 Simmer for 15–18 minutes.

5 Add the fish and cook for a further 2–3 minutes. Check the seasoning and serve in four warmed bowls sprinkled with freshly chopped chives or parsley.

Top tip Dyed smoked haddock tastes no different, but looks so much better in this recipe.

Variation You can use smoked cod in this dish if you can't find smoked haddock. The Points per serving will be 3½.

SALADE NICOISE

11½ Points per recipe

Serve 4

Preparation time: 20 minutes

Cooking time: 20 minutes

Calories per serving: 210

Freezing: not recommended

Salade Niçoise has a delicious combination of ingredients in it and makes a substantial meal in itself.

2 eggs

250 g (9 oz) new potatoes, scrubbed and halved if large

150 g (5½ oz) green beans

150 g (5½ oz) mixed salad leaves

8 olives in brine

1 red onion, sliced

200 g (7 oz) canned tuna in spring water

2 tomatoes, quartered

1 tablespoon olive oil

juice of ½ lemon

½ teaspoon Dijon mustard

salt and freshly ground black pepper

1 Bring a small saucepan of water to the boil and boil the eggs for 8 minutes. Remove the eggs from the pan and run cold water over them for 3–4 minutes to prevent the yolks from turning grey.

2 Cook the potatoes in a medium saucepan of lightly salted, boiling water for 10 minutes and then add the beans. Cook for a further 6–8 minutes until the potatoes and beans are tender. Drain and leave to cool slightly.

3 Shell the eggs and cut them into quarters.

4 In a salad bowl, gently toss together the salad leaves, olives, red onion, potatoes and beans.

5 Drain the tuna and then fork the tuna over the top of the salad and top with the egg quarters and tomatoes.

6 Whisk together the olive oil, lemon juice and Dijon mustard. Season to taste.

7 Pour the dressing over the salad and serve immediately.

Salade Niçoise: A deliciously satisfying salad for 3 Points.

MINESTRONE SOUP

3 POINTS

13 Points per recipe

Serves 4
Preparation time: 20 minutes
Cooking time: 15 minutes
Calories per serving: 265
Freezing: recommended

This soup is a meal in itself with lots of chunky vegetables and pasta for added energy. It makes a satisfying lunchtime meal.

1 teaspoon olive oil
4 rashers of smoked lean back bacon, cut into strips
2 onions, chopped finely
1 celery stick, diced
2 garlic cloves, chopped
100 g (3½ oz) potatoes, diced
1 × 250 g (9 oz) swede, peeled and diced
2 carrots, diced
2 tomatoes, chopped
100 g (3½ oz) small pasta shapes
1.3 litres (2½ pints) vegetable or chicken stock
salt and freshly ground black pepper
freshly chopped parsley, to garnish

1 Heat the oil in a large saucepan and add the bacon and onions. Cook for 4–5 minutes, until the onions are softened.

2 Add the celery, garlic, potatoes, swede, carrots, tomatoes and pasta shapes. Stir thoroughly.

3 Pour in the stock, cover the pan and cook for 15 minutes until the vegetables are soft.

4 Season and serve in four warmed bowls garnished with freshly chopped parsley.

Variation For a vegetarian option omit the bacon and use vegetable stock. The Points will then be reduced to 1½ per serving.

HERBY POTATO SALAD

2½ POINTS

11 Points per recipe

V *Serves 4*
Preparation time: 10 minutes
Cooking time: 12–15 minutes
Calories per serving: 205
Freezing: not recommended

Fresh new potatoes with a dressing full of fresh mint and chives make the perfect accompaniment to a summertime meal.

600 g (1 lb 5 oz) new potatoes, scrubbed and cut in half if large
3 spring onions, sliced
4 tablespoons low fat mayonnaise
1 teaspoon wholegrain mustard
2 carrots, peeled and grated
2 tablespoons chopped fresh mint
1 tablespoon chopped fresh chives
salt and freshly ground black pepper

1 Place the new potatoes in a saucepan of lightly salted water and bring to the boil. Cover and simmer for 12–15 minutes, until the potatoes are tender. Drain and refresh by running under cold water.

2 Place the potatoes in a large bowl and mix in the spring onions, mayonnaise and wholegrain mustard.

3 Finally, gently stir in the grated carrot and freshly chopped herbs.

4 Season well and serve.

Variation Add 50 g (1¾ oz) crispy lean back bacon bits snipped into small pieces for a little American flavour! The Points will then be 3½ per serving.

VEGETABLE PILAFF

12 Points per recipe

Ⓥ Ⓥⓖ *Serves 4*

Preparation time: 30 minutes

Cooking time: 20 minutes

Calories per serving: 265

Freezing: recommended up to 1 month

A delicious and filling vegetarian meal, full of fabulous flavours and vegetables.

low fat cooking spray
1 large onion, chopped
1 garlic clove, crushed
1 leek, sliced
1 red pepper, de-seeded and sliced
1 courgette, sliced
75 g (2³⁄₄ oz) baby sweetcorn, halved
110 g (4 oz) asparagus tips
1 teaspoon ground cumin
1 teaspoon turmeric
a large pinch of saffron threads
180 g (6¹⁄₂ oz) long grain or basmati rice
500 ml (18 fl oz) vegetable stock
30 g (1¹⁄₄ oz) flaked almonds
¹⁄₂ teaspoon chilli powder

1 Spray a very large frying pan with low fat cooking spray. Add the onion, garlic and leek and cook for 3–4 minutes until they start to soften. Add the red pepper, courgette, baby sweetcorn and asparagus and cook for another 3–4 minutes before adding the spices and saffron.

2 Add the rice and stir well to coat everything in the spices.

3 Pour in the stock, bring to a simmer and cover. Simmer for 20 minutes until all the liquid has been absorbed and the rice is cooked.

4 Meanwhile spray a small frying pan with low fat cooking spray and stir fry the flaked almonds and chilli powder for 5–6 minutes until they are golden. Set aside on kitchen paper.

5 When the pilaff is cooked, transfer it to a large serving plate or dish and sprinkle with the spicy almond flakes.

Top tip Make sure the frying pan is covered completely to help the rice to steam – try not to remove the cover for a look too often!

Variations Most No Point vegetables can be used for this dish, try broccoli, cauliflower and celery, or even root vegetables like swede and turnip.

Vegetable Pilaff: Supper with a fabulous flair for just 3 Points.

TURKISH LAMB STEW

9½ Total Points per recipe

Serves 4

Preparation time: 30 minutes

Cooking time: 30–40 minutes

Calories per serving: 220

Freezing: recommended up to 1 month

With lots of vegetables and fresh oregano, this stew gives you a real taste of the Mediterranean. Serve with some No Point Mediterranean vegetables such as courgettes or a crunchy green salad.

low fat cooking spray
270 g (9¼ oz) lean lamb leg, cubed
1 large onion, chopped
1 garlic clove, crushed
100 g (3½ oz) potatoes, diced
400 g can of chopped tomatoes
1 green pepper, sliced

100 g (3½ oz) canned chick peas
1 small aubergine, chopped
1 tablespoon chopped fresh oregano or marjoram
4 black olives, sliced
salt and freshly ground black pepper

1 Spray a large saucepan with low fat cooking spray. Add the lamb and cook to brown it for 4–5 minutes, stirring occasionally.

2 Add the onion and garlic, and cook for another 3–4 minutes.

3 Add the remaining ingredients except for the olives. Add 200 ml (7 fl oz) of water. Bring to a gentle simmer.

4 Stir well, season to taste and cover the pan. Simmer for 30–40 minutes or until the lamb is tender.

5 Uncover the pan and add the olives. Simmer for a further 4–5 minutes and then serve.

Variation For a vegetarian version, you can omit the lamb and replace it with 250 g (9 oz) Quorn – the stew will only need to cook for 15–20 minutes in step 4, instead of 30–40 minutes. The Points will be reduced to 1½ per serving.

PRIMAVERA PASTA

12½ Points per recipe

Ⓥ *Serves 4*

Preparation and cooking time: 25 minutes

Calories per serving: 215

Freezing: not recommended

This fresh tasting pasta dish, with fresh basil and crunchy mange tout peas, is delicious eaten hot or cold.

200 g (7 oz) pasta shapes
2 big handfuls of fresh basil
90 g (3¼ oz) mushrooms
100 g (3½ oz) cherry tomatoes

90 g (3¼ oz) mange tout peas, shredded
1 teaspoon olive oil
salt and freshly ground black pepper
1 tablespoon grated Parmesan cheese, to serve

1 Bring a large saucepan of lightly salted water to the boil. Add the pasta and cook for 8–10 minutes, until just tender.

2 Place the fresh basil, mushrooms and cherry tomatoes in a food processor and blend for a few seconds so the sauce is still quite chunky.

3 When the pasta is cooked, drain and reserve 4 tablespoons of the cooking water.

4 Return the pasta to the pan with the water, basil sauce, mange tout peas and olive oil.

5 Heat, stirring, for 3–4 minutes. Check the seasoning and serve in four bowls. Sprinkle over the grated Parmesan.

SPICY BANANA MUFFINS

24 Points per recipe

Ⓥ Makes 10

Preparation time: 15 minutes

Cooking time: 20–25 minutes

Calories per serving: 165

Freezing: recommended for up to 1 month

A great way to start the day.

50 g (1³/4 oz) low fat spread
200 g (7 oz) plain flour
2 teaspoons baking powder
100 g (3¹/2 oz) caster sugar
1 teaspoon ground cinnamon
2 bananas
juice of 1 lemon
100 ml (3¹/2 fl oz) skimmed milk
1 egg, beaten

1 Preheat the oven to Gas Mark 6/ 200°C/fan oven 180°C. Put 10 paper muffin cases into a muffin tin.

2 Melt the low fat spread and leave to cool slightly.

3 Sift the dry ingredients into a large bowl.

4 Mash the bananas with a fork and 1 teaspoon of the lemon juice.

5 Mix together the remaining lemon juice, milk and egg.

6 Pour the wet ingredients into the dry ones and stir very carefully – do not over mix.

7 Gently fold in the mashed banana and then divide the mixture between the paper muffin cases.

8 Cook in the preheated oven for 20–25 minutes until golden. Cool on a rack or eat slightly warm – delicious!

Top tip The muffin mixture should not be over mixed – don't worry if all the flour doesn't look mixed in.

LEMON ICE CREAM

14 Points per recipe

Ⓥ Serves 6

Preparation time: 10 minutes + 3–4 hours freezing time

Calories per serving: 155

Freezing: recommended

A creamy lemon ice cream to be savoured and enjoyed with friends on a hot summer's day.

450 ml (16 fl oz) low fat custard
150 g (5¹/2 oz) lemon curd
200 ml (7 fl oz) low fat plain yogurt
grated zest of 1 lemon

1 Beat together the custard, lemon curd and yogurt, and then stir in the lemon zest.

2 To make by hand, pour the mixture into a plastic container with a lid and place it in the freezer. (If you have an ice cream maker, place the mixture in it and churn according to the manufacturer's instructions, until frozen.)

3 After 45 minutes take the container out of the freezer. Whisk the contents with a fork, making sure to scrape the frozen mixture from the sides of the container.

4 Repeat this three times and then leave to freeze for about 3 or 4 hours.

Spicy Banana Muffins: Take a break with this tasty muffin for only 2½ Points.

French Apple Tart:
Enjoy a slice of this
impressive dessert
for 3 Points.

FRENCH APPLE TART

18 Points per recipe

Ⓥ Serves 6

Preparation time: 25 minutes +
30 minutes chilling
Cooking time: 30 minutes
Calories per serving: 205
Freezing: not recommended

This is a very simple way of making an apple tart. It looks pretty – and it tastes wonderful.

130 g (4¾ oz) plain white flour, plus
2 teaspoons for rolling

1 teaspoon fruit sugar (fructose)

65 g (2¼ oz) low fat spread

220 ml (7½ fl oz) low fat custard,
ready to serve

3 eating apples

1 teaspoon ground cinnamon

3 tablespoons reduced sugar apricot
jam

1 Preheat the oven to Gas Mark 6/ 200°C/fan oven 180°C.

2 Place the flour and fruit sugar in a bowl. Add the low fat spread and with your fingertips, rub it into the dry ingredients until the mixture resembles fine breadcrumbs.

3 Add approximately 2½ tablespoons of cold water to bind the pastry together. Wrap the pastry in clingfilm and leave it to rest in the fridge for 30 minutes.

4 On a lightly floured surface, roll out the pastry and use it to line a 20 cm (8 inch) loose bottomed flan tin. Prick the surface with a fork and place the flan tin on a baking sheet. Bake in the oven for 15 minutes.

5 Leave the pastry case to cool for 5 minutes then spoon in the custard.

6 Peel, core and cut the apples into quarters and then into slices. Place the slices on top of the custard, arranging them so they are slightly overlapping, until the whole surface is covered.

7 Sprinkle the apples with ground cinnamon.

8 In a small saucepan heat the apricot jam and then pour it over the apples. Return the tart to the oven for another 15 minutes. Serve hot or cold.

Top tip Leaving pastry to rest prevents it from shrinking while baking.

Variation A pear tart can be made in the same way. The Points per serving will remain the same.

RHUBARB FOOL

10½ Points per recipe

Ⓥ Serves 4

Preparation time: 20 minutes +
30 minutes chilling
Cooking time: 15 minutes
Calories per serving: 150
Freezing: not recommended

The white chocolate in this creamy, fruit dessert adds a touch of luxury!

500 g (1 lb 2 oz) fresh rhubarb

2 tablespoons fruit sugar (fructose)

60 g (2 oz) white chocolate

150 ml (5 fl oz) ready to serve low
fat custard

1 Place the rhubarb in a medium saucepan with 3 tablespoons of water and the fruit sugar. Bring to a gentle simmer. Continue to simmer for 12–15 minutes until the rhubarb is soft. Take the pan off the heat and leave to cool.

2 Meanwhile, melt the white chocolate in a large bowl over a saucepan of barely simmering water. Remove the bowl from the heat.

3 Beat the custard into the melted white chocolate.

4 Gently stir the rhubarb into the custard mixture, not combining it completely.

5 Spoon the fool into glasses or individual dishes and chill in the fridge for at least 30 minutes until ready to serve.

Top tip Rhubarb does vary a lot in sweetness – taste the cooked rhubarb before adding the custard to check whether it is sweet enough. If not, try adding a little more fruit sugar, remembering to alter the Points accordingly. Remember it will become sweeter when combined with the custard and white chocolate.

4 Points
and under

This chapter is full of wonderful recipes for only 3¹/₂–4 Points with lots of family favourites included. You'll find a fantastic selection of delicious main meals which you can happily share with others and even some scrummy puddings and home baked scones – perfect for those days when you really fancy a tasty treat.

SPAGHETTI BOLOGNESE

16¹/₂ Points per recipe
Serves 4
Preparation time: 15 minutes
Cooking time: 35 minutes
Calories per serving: 330
Freezing: not recommended

This version is much lower in Points than the traditional family favourite – but no one will ever guess!

low fat cooking spray
1 green pepper, de-seeded and diced
1 onion, diced
1 garlic clove, chopped
225 g (8 oz) extra lean beef mince
1 courgette, diced
1 large carrot, diced
150 g (3¹/₂ oz) chestnut mushrooms
400 g can of chopped tomatoes

2 tablespoons tomato purée
1 tablespoon chopped fresh marjoram
180 g (6¹/₂ oz) dried spaghetti
salt and freshly ground black pepper
2 tablespoons chopped fresh basil, to serve

1 Spray a large saucepan with low fat cooking spray and add the green pepper, onion and garlic. Fry for 3–4 minutes, stirring occasionally, until they start to soften.

2 Add the minced beef and fry for a further 6–8 minutes to brown the meat, stirring from time to time.

3 Add the courgette, carrot, mushrooms, canned tomatoes, tomato purée, marjoram and seasoning. Stir well before adding 200 ml (7 fl oz) of water. Stir again and bring to a simmer. Simmer for 20 minutes.

4 Bring a large saucepan of lightly salted water to the boil. Add the spaghetti and cook for 10–12 minutes until just tender.

5 Drain the spaghetti and divide between four warmed plates or pasta bowls and spoon over the Bolognese sauce. Sprinkle with the chopped basil and serve immediately.

Variation Try using chicken or turkey mince for a change. The Points per serving will be 3½.

Spaghetti Bolognese:
Tuck in to a generous
helping of this
fantastic Italian
classic for only
4 Points.

1 Heat the oil in a medium pan and stir fry the lemongrass, ginger and garlic for 2–3 minutes.

2 Add the chicken and stir fry for 5–6 minutes before adding the butternut squash and Thai curry paste. Stir well to coat the chicken and vegetables with the flavourings.

3 Pour in the chicken stock and bring to a simmer. Cook for 15 minutes.

4 Add the coconut milk, spinach and spring onions. Simmer for a further 4–5 minutes to heat everything through and wilt the spinach.

5 Season to taste and serve sprinkled with toasted, flaked almonds.

Top tip The outer leaves of lemongrass can be very tough, always remove a few layers before chopping or slicing the inside.

Variation This soup could be made with 175 g (6 oz) prawns instead of the chicken – add it in step 2 with the butternut squash. The Points will be reduced to 2½ per serving.

Thai Chicken Soup: A comforting and aromatic soup for 3½ Points.

THAI CHICKEN SOUP

14 Points per recipe
Serves 4
Preparation time: 20 minutes
Cooking time: 25 minutes
Calories per serving: 250
Freezing: not recommended

With the fragrant flavours of Thailand and the creaminess of coconut milk, this soup is hard to resist!

1 teaspoon olive oil

1 stick of lemongrass, chopped

1 cm (½ inch) fresh ginger, peeled and chopped finely

2 garlic cloves, crushed

2 skinless medium chicken breasts, sliced into strips

1 small butternut squash, de-seeded, peeled and diced

1 teaspoon Thai curry paste

850 ml (1½ pints) chicken stock

100 ml (3½ fl oz) low fat coconut milk

125 g (4½ oz) baby spinach

3 spring onions, sliced finely

salt and freshly ground black pepper

3 tablespoons flaked almonds, toasted

CAESAR SALAD

14½ Points per recipe

Serves 4
Preparation time: 15 minutes
Calories per serving: 150
Freezing: not recommended

Caesar salad is a great American invention – lots of crunchy salad leaves with a creamy, luxurious dressing.

10 cashew nuts
50 g (1¾ oz) canned anchovies, drained
100 g (3½ oz) low fat mayonnaise
50 ml (2 fl oz) low fat plain yogurt
juice of ½ lemon
2 garlic cloves, crushed
1 teaspoon Dijon mustard
2 romaine lettuce
30 g (1¼ oz) grated Parmesan cheese
salt and freshly ground black pepper

1 Toast the cashew nuts under the grill until they are golden.
2 Chop half the anchovies roughly, leaving the remainder whole.
3 Place the mayonnaise, yogurt, lemon juice, garlic and mustard in a blender or food processor and blend well.
4 Stir the chopped anchovies into this dressing and check the seasoning.
5 Roughly tear the romaine leaves and place them in a bowl. Pour over the salad dressing and toss the lettuce gently.
6 Scatter the salad with the toasted cashew nuts, sprinkle with grated Parmesan cheese and decorate with the whole anchovies.

Variation If you have some leftover cooked chicken (175 g/6 oz), flake it and add this to the salad to make a substantial lunchtime dish. The Points will be 4½ per serving.

LIVER WITH MASH

8 Points per recipe

Serves 2
Preparation time: 20 minutes
Cooking time: 30 minutes
Calories per serving: 200
Freezing: not recommended

Creamy mustard mash and caramelised onions topped with succulent pieces of herby liver – delicious!

low fat cooking spray
2 onions, sliced thinly
2 garlic cloves, sliced thinly
½ tablespoon balsamic vinegar
200 g (7 oz) potatoes, peeled and chopped
1 tablespoon half fat crème fraîche
½ teaspoon wholegrain mustard
1 teaspoon low fat spread
100 g (3½ oz) liver, cut into strips
1 tablespoon chopped fresh sage
salt and freshly ground black pepper

1 First make the onion marmalade. Spray a small saucepan with low fat cooking spray. Add the onions and garlic and cook over a low heat for 10 minutes, stirring from time to time. Add the balsamic vinegar and continue to cook and stir for another 10 minutes.
2 For the mash, cook the potatoes in a large saucepan of lightly salted, boiling water until tender. Drain. Add the crème fraîche and mustard, and mash with a potato masher or fork. Season and keep warm.
3 Heat the low fat spread in a small frying pan and add the liver. Stir fry over a high heat for 4–5 minutes until the liver is cooked. Sprinkle with the sage.
4 Divide the mashed potatoes between two plates – place a spoonful of mashed potatoes in the middle of each plate and then press it down. Top with a spoonful of onion marmalade and then spoon over the liver with the pan juices.
5 Season and serve.

Top tip Try not to over cook the liver or it will become tough.

Chicken with Ratatouille: A quick and easy supper with wonderful Mediterranean flavours for 4 Points.

CHICKEN WITH RATATOUILLE

7¹/₂ Points per recipe

Serves 2

Preparation time: 15 minutes

Cooking time: 20 minutes

Calories per serving: 290

Freezing: recommended for up to 1 month

Stuffing chicken breasts helps to keep them moist and adds extra flavour to the meat.

60 g (2 oz) low fat garlic and herb soft cheese (e.g. Boursin Light)

1 spring onion, chopped

2 medium skinless chicken breasts

600 ml (20 fl oz) chicken stock

For the ratatouille

low fat cooking spray

1 small onion, chopped

1 red pepper, de-seeded and chopped

1 courgette, sliced

227 g can of chopped tomatoes

salt and freshly ground black pepper

1 In a small bowl mix together the soft cheese and spring onion.

2 Wrap each chicken breast in a large piece of clingfilm. Apply pressure with a rolling pin to make the breast thinner. Open the clingfilm, place half the cheese mixture on the chicken breast and roll it up. Wrap the breast up tightly in the clingfilm.

3 Put the chicken stock in a medium saucepan and bring to a simmer. Place the stuffed, wrapped breasts in the stock. Simmer for 15 minutes.

4 Meanwhile, make the ratatouille. Spray a small saucepan with low fat cooking spray. Add the onion and pepper and cook for 2–3 minutes before adding the remaining ingredients. Simmer for 12–15 minutes.

5 When the chicken breasts are cooked, remove them from the stock and leave to cool slightly before unwrapping. Slice the chicken.

6 Divide the ratatouille and slices of chicken between two warmed plates.

BALSAMIC LAMB

8 Points per recipe

Serves 2

Preparation and cooking time: 15 minutes + 30 minutes marinating

Calories per serving: 280

Freezing: not recommended

This is great for a quick supper as it doesn't require too much preparation. You can just leave the lamb marinating while you prepare any vegetables you wish. Mange tout peas are particularly delicious with this.

2 tablespoons balsamic vinegar

2 tablespoons chopped fresh thyme

2 tablespoons chopped fresh rosemary

200 g (7 oz) lean lamb leg steaks

4 teaspoons olive oil

2 tablespoons chopped fresh mint

salt and freshly ground black pepper

1 In a shallow dish mix together the balsamic vinegar, thyme, rosemary and seasoning. Place the lamb in the mixture, turning to coat them in the marinade. Leave to marinate in the fridge for 30 minutes.

2 Preheat the grill.

3 Place the lamb under the grill and cook, turning twice, for 6–8 minutes, depending on how pink you like your lamb.

4 Heat the remaining marinade in a small saucepan or in the microwave. Whisk in the olive oil and the chopped mint.

5 Serve the lamb with the herb dressing poured over the top.

Top tip Never marinate in metal containers, always use china – and always keep marinades in the fridge.

Variation Try any other of your favourite herbs for the marinade.

1 Preheat the oven to Gas Mark 6/ 200°C/fan oven 180°C.

2 Spray a medium saucepan with low fat cooking spray and add the leeks and quartered mushrooms. Cover and leave them to sweat for 15 minutes, stirring occasionally.

3 Remove the pan from the heat and leave to cool slightly.

4 Place one sheet of filo pastry on the work surface. Spray it with low fat cooking spray and then lay another sheet on top and spray again. Repeat this until all the sheets are used.

5 Add the chives, Stilton cheese and seasoning to the leek and mushroom mixture and mix well.

6 Spoon the cheese and leek mixture down the centre of the stack of filo pastry sheets. Tuck the sides in and roll the pastry up, completely sealing the mixture in.

7 Place the strudel on a baking sheet with the join underneath and spray it with low fat cooking spray.

8 Cook in the oven for 20 minutes or until golden.

9 Meanwhile, spray a small saucepan with low fat cooking spray and add the onion and diced mushrooms. Stir fry for 5–6 minutes before adding the remaining ingredients. Check the seasoning.

10 When the strudel is cooked, remove it from the oven and cut it into four slices. Serve each portion with a spoonful of sauce.

Variation If you prefer a meat version, try replacing the cheese with 60 g (2 oz) grilled lean back bacon bits. The Points will be reduced to 2½ per serving.

Stilton, Mushroom and Leek Strudel: Each deliciously cheesey slice is just 4 Points.

STILTON, MUSHROOM AND LEEK STRUDEL

4 POINTS

15½ Points per recipe

 Serves 4

Preparation time: 30 minutes

Cooking time: 20 minutes

Calories per serving: 230

Freezing: not recommended

This impressive vegetarian dish is a meal in itself. It's delicious served with a fresh, colourful salad.

low fat cooking spray

2 leeks, sliced

300 g (10½ oz) chestnut mushrooms, quartered

5 sheets of filo pastry

2 tablespoons chopped fresh chives,

80 g (3 oz) Stilton cheese, crumbled

1 small onion, diced

200 g (7 oz) chestnut mushrooms, diced

2 tablespoons half fat crème fraîche

1½ teaspoons wholegrain mustard

1 tablespoon chopped fresh parsley

salt and freshly ground black pepper

CHEESE AND CELERY SCONES

40½ Points per recipe

Ⓥ Makes 12

Preparation and cooking time:
25 minutes

Calories per serving: 195

Freezing: recommended up to 1 month

These scones are delicious straight out of the oven with a spread of low fat cream cheese, but remember to add the extra Points! Alternatively, keep them in an airtight container for when friends pop by.

450 g (1 lb) self raising white flour plus 1 teaspoon for rolling

1 teaspoon salt

2 teaspoons baking powder

75 g (2¾ oz) low fat spread

150 g (5½ oz) half fat Cheddar cheese, grated

1 celery stick, diced

300 ml (10 fl oz) semi skimmed milk

1 Preheat the oven to Gas Mark 7/ 220°C/fan oven 200°C.

2 Sift the flour, salt and baking powder into a large bowl.

3 Using your fingertips, rub the low fat spread into the flour mixture until it resembles fine breadcrumbs.

4 Stir in the grated cheese and celery.

5 Pour in the milk and mix gently so that you have a soft, loose dough – be sure not to over mix.

6 Turn out the dough on to a floured work surface and then roll it out to about 2 cm (¾ inch) thick. Cut out 12 rounds with a biscuit cutter and place them on a baking sheet.

7 Cook in the oven for 8–10 minutes, until golden and risen. Remove from the oven and place them on a cooling rack until cool.

Top tip These scones can be made in the food processor: place the dry ingredients in the food processor, add the low fat spread and blend for a few seconds. Stir in the cheese and celery, add the milk and blend again. Continue from step 6.

Variations Try using 80 g (3 oz) blue cheese with chopped cherry tomatoes or spring onions instead of Cheddar and celery. The Points per scone will remain the same.

CRUNCHIE COINTREAU CREAMS

16 Points per recipe

Ⓥ Serves 4

Preparation time: 15 minutes +
30 minutes chilling

Calories per serving: 195

Freezing: not recommended

This is a slight twist on tiramisu – an orange version instead of the traditional coffee for those who want to try something a little different!

1 teaspoon Cointreau liqueur

grated zest and juice of 1 orange

8 sponge fingers

200 ml (7 fl oz) low fat plain yogurt

150 ml (5 fl oz) half fat crème fraîche

1 Crunchie bar

1 In a shallow bowl, mix together the Cointreau and orange juice.

2 Break each sponge finger in half and dip in the orange juice mixture, allowing it to soak briefly. Place the sponge fingers in the bottom of four glasses or individual glass dishes. Pour over any remaining liquid.

3 Mix together the yogurt, crème fraîche and orange zest.

4 Spoon the yogurt mixture over the sponge fingers.

5 Smash the Crunchie bar with a rolling pin while it is still in its wrapper. Sprinkle the crumbs on top of each dessert.

6 Chill the desserts for at least 20 minutes and up to 30 minutes before serving.

Variation For a quick tiramisu, replace the Cointreau with Tia Maria and the orange juice with strong coffee. Sprinkle the top with 2 teaspoons of cocoa powder instead of the Crunchie bar. The Points will be reduced to 3 per serving.

Queen of Puddings: The name says it all! Dish up this luxurious dessert for only 4 Points.

QUEEN OF PUDDINGS

 4 POINTS

25½ Points per recipe

ⓥ *Serves 6*

Preparation time: 25 minutes +
15 minutes standing

Cooking time: 45–50 minutes

Calories per serving: 270

Freezing: not recommended

The different textured layers and oozing jam in this very traditional pudding make it hard to resist. Don't worry – it's still low in Points!

600 ml (20 fl oz) semi skimmed milk
25 g (1 oz) low fat spread
grated zest of 1 lemon
4 large eggs, separated
100 g (3½ oz) caster sugar
150 g (5½ oz) fresh white breadcrumbs
low fat cooking spray
2½ tablespoons reduced sugar jam

1 Preheat the oven to Gas Mark 4/ 180°C/fan oven 160°C.

2 Warm the milk, low fat spread and lemon zest in a medium saucepan.

3 Whisk in the egg yolks and 2 teaspoons of the caster sugar to make a custard.

4 Place the breadcrumbs in a bowl and pour the custard over them. Mix thoroughly.

5 Spray a 1.2 litre (2 pint) shallow ovenproof dish with low fat cooking spray. Pour the breadcrumb mixture into it and leave it to stand for 15 minutes.

6 Bake in the oven for 25–30 minutes until just set – it should still be wobbly in the middle. Remove from the oven.

7 Warm the jam and spread it over the pudding.

8 Whisk the egg whites until stiff and then gradually add all the remaining sugar. Continue to whisk until you have a stiff and glossy meringue mixture.

9 Pile the meringue mixture on top of the pudding and return it to the oven for 15–20 minutes, until the meringue is cooked and golden.

Top tip Always make sure the bowl you are whisking the egg whites in is completely free of grease or the whites will not whisk to a thick consistency.

Variation Try using other flavours of reduced sugar jam to make this pudding.

BREAD AND PEACH PUDDING

 3½ POINTS

13 Points per recipe

ⓥ *Serves 4*

Preparation time: 15 minutes

Cooking time: 40 minutes

Calories per serving: 210

Freezing: not recommended

A unique and very tasty version of a much loved classic.

low fat cooking spray
3 thick slices of brown bread
410 g (14¼ oz) canned peaches in juice
2 tablespoons mixed dried fruit
200 ml (7 fl oz) semi skimmed milk
2 eggs, beaten
½ teaspoon ground nutmeg
2 teaspoons muscovado sugar

1 Preheat the oven to Gas Mark 4/ 180°C/fan oven 160°C.

2 Spray a medium size shallow ovenproof dish with low fat cooking spray.

3 Break up the slices of bread and place them in the dish.

4 Drain the peaches, reserving the juice and chop them roughly. Place them in the dish with the bread. Sprinkle over the mixed dried fruit.

5 Whisk together the reserved juice, milk and eggs and pour this over the bread and fruit.

6 Sprinkle the top with the nutmeg and muscovado sugar and bake in the oven for 40 minutes, until golden.

Variation Most fruits work well in this recipe – try tinned pears or apricots for a change. The Points will remain the same.

Bread and Peach Pudding: Try something different for 3½ Points.

5 Points
and under

You'll love the recipes in this chapter; there is something here for everyone to enjoy. We've included low Point versions of many of your favourite dishes and the flavours are fantastic. Be sure to find the time in your busy lifestyle for cooking – you'll make yourself feel great!

CHICKEN PAD THAI

18 Points per recipe
Serves 4
Preparation and cooking time:
35–40 minutes
Calories per serving: 350
Freezing: not recommended

Pad Thai is such a favourite Thai dish and this version can be enjoyed without using up your daily Point allowance!

125 g (4½ oz) rice noodles

low fat cooking spray

2 garlic cloves, crushed

2 cm (¾ inch) fresh ginger, peeled and chopped finely

1 egg, beaten

2 medium skinless chicken breasts, cut into strips

3 spring onions, chopped

½ teaspoon chilli flakes

125 g (4½ oz) fresh beansprouts

2 carrots, peeled and grated

3 tablespoons soy sauce

50 g (1¾ oz) dry roasted peanuts, crushed roughly

1 Place the noodles in a large bowl and cover them with boiling water. Leave to stand for 4 minutes, and then drain and refresh them with cold water. Leave to one side.

2 Spray a wok or large frying pan with low fat cooking spray and heat it. When it is quite hot add the garlic, ginger and the egg.

3 Using chopsticks or a wooden spatula, move the egg around to scramble it until it is cooked. Remove the mixture from the pan and keep to one side.

4 Spray the wok or pan with low fat cooking spray and add the chicken strips. Stir fry for 8–10 minutes, and then add the spring onions and chilli flakes. Stir fry for another 2–3 minutes.

5 Add the noodles and all but 4 tablespoons of beansprouts and the grated carrots. Continue to stir fry for 3–4 minutes. Add the soy and all but 2 tablespoons of dry roasted peanuts. Stir fry for 3–4 minutes more.

6 Serve sprinkled with the remaining beansprouts and peanuts.

Top tips Soy sauce is quite salty, so this recipe does not require any other seasoning.

Using chopsticks to cook with is much easier for this recipe, it helps to separate the noodles when stir frying.

Variation For a non meat version you can either omit the chicken or replace it with 250 g (9 oz) prawns. The Points per serving will be 3½ without the chicken and 4 with the prawns.

Chicken Pad Thai: The dish we all love for 4½ Points.

Chicken Masala:
Make it Indian
tonight for only
5 Points.

CHICKEN MASALA

20½ Points per recipe

Serves 4

Preparation time: 15 minutes

Cooking time: 20–25 minutes

Calories per serving: 335

Freezing: recommended for up to 1 month

This is a delicious, creamy curry that will happily replace the Friday night take away!

1 teaspoon cumin seeds

1 teaspoon mustard seeds

1 onion, grated

2–3 garlic cloves, crushed

2 cm (¾ inch) fresh ginger, peeled and grated

2 teaspoons ground cumin

2 teaspoons turmeric

2 teaspoons curry powder

1 teaspoons paprika

1 small aubergine, diced

2 tablespoons tomato purée

3 medium skinless chicken breasts, cut into bite size pieces

200 ml (7 fl oz) chicken stock

200 ml (7 fl oz) low fat coconut milk

2 tablespoons chopped fresh coriander

300 g (10½ oz) cooked rice, to serve

1 Heat a non stick large frying pan and add the cumin seeds and mustard seeds.

2 When the mustard seeds start to pop add the onion, garlic and ginger. Stir well.

3 Add the remaining spices and stir to mix the flavours together.

4 Add the aubergine, tomato purée and the chicken pieces. Stir to coat everything well.

5 Pour over the chicken stock and coconut milk and then bring to a simmer. Continue to simmer for 15–20 minutes, until the chicken is cooked.

6 Add the coconut milk and stir until the sauce thickens.

7 Finally add the chopped coriander and serve with freshly cooked rice.

Variation For a vegetarian option, omit the chicken and add 1 kg (2 lb 4 oz) potatoes instead. This will reduce the cooking time to 10–15 minutes. The Points per serving will be 6.

MEXICAN HAM AND BEAN SOUP

18 Points per recipe

Serves 4

Preparation time: 10 minutes

Cooking time: 20 minutes

Calories per serving: 255

Freezing: recommended up to 1 month

A hearty, spicy soup, which can be spiced up more if you wish – just add more chilli powder and you could be on your way to Mexico!

low fat cooking spray

1 large onion, chopped

200 g (7 oz) ham, cut into short strips

50 g (1¾ oz) dried split red lentils

400 g can of flageolet beans, drained and rinsed

410 g can of cannellini beans, drained and rinsed

1–2 teaspoons chilli powder

1.2 litres (2 pints) vegetable stock

1 tablespoon tomato purée

salt and freshly ground black pepper

1 tablespoon chopped fresh parsley, to serve

1 Spray a medium saucepan with low fat cooking spray. Add the onion and ham and cook for 6–8 minutes, stirring occasionally, until the onion starts to soften.

2 Pour in the lentils and drained beans, and then stir in the chilli powder to coat all the vegetables.

3 Pour in the stock and add the tomato purée. Stir well and then bring to a simmer. Continue to simmer for 20 minutes.

4 Leave to cool slightly and then remove 3–4 cups of the soup and blend this in a food processor or blender. Return the blended soup to the pan and check the seasoning.

5 Serve in four warmed bowls sprinkled with chopped parsley.

Top tip Canned beans and pulses are so easy and quick to use as, unlike the dried ones, they do not require any soaking overnight.

Variation For a vegetarian bean soup just omit the ham. The Points will then be 3½ per serving.

2 Preheat the oven to Gas Mark 6/ 200°C/fan oven 180°C.

3 Shape the mince mixture into small balls – it should make 12.

4 Spray a frying pan with low fat cooking spray and gently brown the meatballs, turning occasionally to brown them all over.

5 Remove the meatballs from the pan and place them in a casserole dish.

6 Add the mango chutney and 4 tablespoons of water to the frying pan and cook for 1 minute, stirring to gather all the bits from the pan.

7 Pour this mixture over the meatballs. Cover and cook for 15–20 minutes until they are cooked through.

8 Serve three meatballs per person with the sauce spooned over.

Spicy Swedish Meatballs: Satisfaction guaranteed for 5 Points.

SPICY SWEDISH MEATBALLS

20 Points per recipe

Serves 4

Preparation: 20 minutes

Cooking time: 15–20 minutes

Calories per serving: 270

Freezing: not recommended

This recipe is based on an original Swedish recipe for spicy meatballs with a sweet sauce. Serve with a No Point green vegetable such as cooked, shredded cabbage.

500 g (1 lb 2 oz) extra lean minced beef

1 small onion, chopped finely

2 garlic cloves, chopped finely

1½ tablespoons chopped fresh dill

1 egg, beaten

1 teaspoon Worcestershire sauce

2 tablespoons tomato purée

low fat cooking spray

2 tablespoons mango chutney

salt and freshly ground black pepper

1 In a bowl, mix together the minced beef, onion, garlic, dill, egg, Worcestershire sauce, tomato purée and seasoning – this is easier to do with your hands, squeezing all the ingredients together.

SUMMER PASTA

 4½ POINTS

8½ Total Points per recipe
Serves 2
Preparation time: 15 minutes
Cooking time: 15 minutes
Calories per serving: 320
Freezing: not recommended

Fresh peas and mint put you in mind of summer – try this recipe to get you in the mood!

100 g (3½ oz) penne pasta
3 tablespoons frozen or fresh peas
100 g (3½ oz) mange tout peas, shredded
1 bunch of fresh mint, leaves only, chopped
low fat cooking spray
100 g (3½ oz) ham, cut into strips
1 teaspoon olive oil
salt and freshly ground black pepper

1 Cook the pasta in a medium saucepan of lightly salted, boiling water for 10–12 minutes.

2 Meanwhile bring a small saucepan of water to the boil and add the peas, mange tout peas and half the mint. Cook for 3–4 minutes. Drain and set aside.

3 Spray a small frying pan with low fat cooking spray and cook the ham, turning occasionally, until it is golden.

4 When the pasta is cooked, drain and return it to the pan. Add the cooked peas, mint, mange tout peas, ham and olive oil. Shred or chop the remaining mint and add this to the pan. Check the seasoning and serve immediately.

Variation To serve this as a cold salad, refresh both the pasta and the peas after cooking with cold water. Stir in the remaining ingredients as in step 4.

Summer Pasta: 4½ Points for the ideal summer supper.

YOGURT FETA HERB DIP

10 Points per recipe

 Serves 2

Preparation time: 10 minutes

Calories per serving: 250

Freezing: not recommended

A quick creamy, cheese dip with lots of fresh summer herbs.

---

50 g (1³/₄ oz) feta cheese

125 ml (4 fl oz) low fat plain yogurt

1 tablespoon chopped fresh mint

1 tablespoon chopped fresh chives

1 tablespoon chopped fresh oregano

salt and freshly ground black pepper

2 pitta breads

---

1 Crumble the feta into a medium bowl.

2 Mix in the yogurt and herbs and add some seasoning.

3 Grill the pitta breads and cut them into strips.

4 Serve the dip in a bowl with the grilled pitta breads.

Variation If you want to reduce the Points then replace the pitta breads with No Point crunchy crudités such as celery or carrots. The Points per serving will then be 2½.

MOROCCAN VEGETABLE STEW

20½ Points per recipe

Ⓥ Ⓥᴳ Serves 4

Preparation time: 15 minutes

Cooking time: 20 minutes

Calories per serving: 445

Freezing: recommended for the stew only, for up to 1 month

A very flavourful but wholesome dish, with a slightly sweet taste.

---

low fat cooking spray

1 onion, chopped

1 large butternut squash, peeled and chopped

1 sweet potato, peeled and chopped

1 red pepper, de-seeded and sliced

1 aubergine, chopped

1 teaspoon ground ginger

1 teaspoon ground cumin

1 teaspoon ground cinnamon

½ teaspoon chilli flakes

300 ml (½ pint) vegetable stock

400 g can of chopped tomatoes

420 g can of red kidney beans, drained

50 g (1³/₄ oz) raisins

200 g (7 oz) couscous

salt

---

1 Spray a large pan with low fat cooking spray. Add the onion, butternut squash, sweet potato, red pepper and aubergine.

2 Stir well then add the spices and chilli flakes and stir again. Cover and cook on a very low heat for 5–6 minutes.

3 Add the stock, tomatoes, kidney beans and raisins and bring to the boil. Cover and simmer for 20–25 minutes until the vegetables are tender. Meanwhile, prepare the couscous according to the pack instructions.

4 Add salt to taste and serve with the couscous.

APPLE AND RASPBERRY FILO TART

18½ Points per recipe

Ⓥ *Serves 4*

Preparation time: 15 minutes

Cooking time: 20–25 minutes

Calories per serving: 275

Freezing: not recommended

---

800 g (1 lb 11 oz) cooking apples, peeled, cored and sliced

100 ml (3½ fl oz) orange juice

15 sheets of 28½ cm × 43½ cm filo pastry

low fat cooking spray

100 g (3½ oz) fresh raspberries

1 teaspoon icing sugar, to dust

2 tablespoons half fat crème fraîche

1 Heat the oven to Gas Mark 6/ 200°C/fan oven 180°C.

2 In a saucepan, simmer the apples in the orange juice for 8–10 minutes, until just tender.

3 Spray six sheets of filo pastry with low fat spray and use to cover the base of a 23 cm (9 inch) loose bottomed tart tin. Cook in the oven for 5 mins.

4 Remove the tart tin from the oven and fill with the apples and raspberries, but don't add too much juice.

5 Spray the remaining sheets of filo then scrunch them up and arrange on the top of the fruit.

6 Bake for another 15–20 minutes until golden brown.

7 Dust with icing sugar and serve each portion with ½ tablespoon of half fat crème fraîche.

CHOCOLATE TRIFLE

19 Points per recipe

Ⓥ *Serves 4*

Preparation time: 10 minutes

Calories per serving: 405

Freezing: not recommended

---

4 Weight Watchers Double Chocolate Chip muffins, sliced

200 g (7 oz) canned pitted black cherries in syrup

2 teaspoons orange flavoured liqueur (Grand Marnier or Cointreau)

4 chocolate orange Weight Watchers from Heinz Fromage Frais

grated rind of 1 orange

1 Divide the sliced chocolate muffins between four ramekins.

2 Drain the cherries and reserve the syrup. Top the muffins in the ramekins with the cherries and then pour over the syrup.

3 Stir each chocolate orange fromage frais to mix well then pour over the cherries.

4 Top with the grated orange rind and chill until ready to serve.

Banoffee Pie: A devilish dessert for just 5 Points.

BANOFFEE PIE

29 Points per recipe

ⓥ *Serves 6*

Preparation time: 15 minutes +
35 minutes chilling

Calories per serving: 166

Freezing: not recommended

A deliciously indulgent low Point
dessert!

40 g (1½ oz) low fat spread

135 g (4¾ oz) reduced fat digestive
biscuits, crushed

low fat cooking spray

1 butterscotch Angel Delight No
Added Sugar

300 ml (10 fl oz) semi skimmed milk

2 bananas, chopped

200 ml (7 fl oz) low fat plain bio
yogurt

3 teaspoons muscovado sugar

1 Melt the low fat spread in a small
saucepan. Add the crushed biscuits
and mix well.

2 Spray a 20 cm (8 inch) loose
bottomed flan tin with low fat
cooking spray. Pour the crumb
mixture into the tin and press it
down well, right up to the edges.

3 Leave the flan tin in the fridge for
30 minutes.

4 Make up the butterscotch Angel
Delight with the milk according to
the pack instructions. After leaving
for 2 minutes, spoon it over the
biscuit base and return it to the
fridge for 4 minutes or until set.

5 Top with the chopped bananas
and then the yogurt.

6 Sprinkle with muscovado sugar
and return to the fridge for 2 minutes
until the sugar starts to dissolve.
Serve the pie cut into six wedges.

Top tip The biscuit base can be made
well in advance and then you can
complete the dessert just before you
require it.

Variation Try using different flavours
of Angel Delight with different fruits
– try strawberry flavour, topped with
150 g (5½ oz) of fresh strawberries,
sliced. The Points will then be 4½
per serving.

6 Points
and under

These recipes for 5½–6 Points are ideal as your main meal of the day, or as an extra special sweet treat. Some of them are perfect for dinner parties too, and your guests will be completely unaware that you are counting Points!

PEAR AND CHOCOLATE CAKE

45 Points per recipe

V *Makes 8 slices*
Preparation time: 10 minutes
Cooking time: 45–50 minutes
Calories per serving: 295
Freezing: not recommended

If you are in need of a chocolate fix, this will certainly do the job! It has to be one of the easiest cakes you will ever make, and one of the most delicious you have ever tasted!

low fat cooking spray

150 g (5½ oz) plain white flour

1 teaspoon baking powder

50 g (1¾ oz) fruit sugar

150 g (5½ oz) low fat spread

3 eggs

150 g (5½ oz) dark chocolate, chopped roughly

1 pear, peeled and diced

1 Preheat the oven to Gas Mark 4/ 180°C/fan oven 160°C. Spray a 900 g (2 lb) loaf tin with low fat cooking spray and line the bottom with greaseproof paper.

2 Place the flour, baking powder, fruit sugar and low fat spread into a food processor and blend for 3–4 seconds to mix them together. Add the eggs and blend for another 6–8 seconds.

3 Stir in the chocolate and the pear, and pour the mixture into the prepared tin.

4 Bake for 45–50 minutes until risen and golden, and a knife comes out clean (apart from melted chocolate).

5 Place the cake on to a cooling rack until cool.

Top tip To prevent making a mess when chopping chocolate, try bashing it with a rolling pin while it is still in its foil wrapper – you can feel how small the pieces are before opening it.

Variation You can use milk chocolate if you prefer, and maybe try making the cake with another fruit such as a mango or a cooking apple. The Points will remain the same.

Pear and Chocolate Cake: Each incredibly delicious slice with rich, oozing chocolate is only 5½ Points.

Creamy Salmon Pasta: The perfect after work supper for 5½ Points.

CREAMY SALMON PASTA

11½ Points per recipe
Serves 2
Preparation time: 10 minutes
Cooking time: 15 minutes
Calories per serving: 360
Freezing: not recommended

A deliciously creamy pasta dish with slivers of smoked salmon and crunchy broccoli florets.

90 g (3¼ oz) fusilli pasta
100 g (3½ oz) broccoli, cut into florets
150 g (5½ oz) salmon fillet
grated zest of 1 lemon
1 tablespoon half fat crème fraîche
4 tablespoons skimmed milk
½ pack of fresh dill, chopped
30 g (1¼ oz) smoked salmon, shredded
salt and freshly ground black pepper

1 Bring a medium saucepan of lightly salted water to the boil. Add the pasta and cook for 5 minutes. Add the broccoli and cook for another 6–7 minutes.

2 Season the salmon fillet and grill for 3–4 minutes on both sides. Flake the cooked salmon, discarding the skin.

3 When the pasta and broccoli are cooked, drain and return them to the pan with the lemon zest, crème fraîche, milk, dill, smoked salmon and cooked, flaked salmon. Mix well and check the seasoning. Serve immediately in two warmed bowls.

Top tip Remember to lightly salt the water you are boiling the pasta in, as this will help to bring out the flavour.

Variation Two medium chicken breasts can be exchanged for the salmon. Cut the breasts into thin strips and then pan fry with low fat cooking spray for 8–10 minutes. Add the chicken to the recipe in step 3. The Points will remain the same.

CHICKEN FLORENTINE

23 Points per recipe
Serves 4
Preparation time: 25 minutes
Cooking time: 20 minutes
Calories per serving: 335
Freezing: not recommended

Eggs Florentine is a traditional Italian dish made with creamy spinach, topped with a poached egg – in this version the spinach is topped with chicken.

500 ml (18 fl oz) chicken stock
4 medium skinless chicken breasts
400 g (14 oz) frozen spinach
a pinch of nutmeg
30 g (1¼ oz) butter
2 tablespoons plain white flour
200 ml (7 fl oz) semi skimmed milk
15 g (½ oz) grated Parmesan cheese
salt and freshly ground black pepper

1 Put the chicken stock in a medium saucepan and bring to the boil. Add the chicken and poach for 15 minutes.

2 Meanwhile, heat the frozen spinach in a medium saucepan, and add the nutmeg and seasoning. Drain well and then spoon this over the base of a shallow ovenproof dish.

3 Melt the butter in a small saucepan and then take it off the heat. Stir in the flour to make a smooth paste. Place the pan back on the heat, gradually add the milk and 2 tablespoons of the chicken stock from the other pan. Stir continuously until it comes to the boil and you have a smooth thick roux sauce. Season well.

4 Pour two thirds of the sauce over the spinach and gently mix it in.

5 Using a slotted spoon, remove the chicken breasts from the saucepan and place them on top of the spinach. Pour over the remaining white sauce.

6 Preheat the grill. Sprinkle the top of the dish with Parmesan cheese and place it under a preheated grill for 5–6 minutes until golden and bubbling. Serve immediately.

Top tip When making a roux sauce do not be tempted to do anything else – it needs to be stirred constantly to prevent lumps!

Variation If you want make the original recipe of Eggs Florentine just substitute the chicken breasts with four large poached eggs and continue the recipe in the same way. The Points will then be 5 per serving.

TUNA LASAGNE

24 Points per recipe

Serves 4

Preparation time: 35 minutes

Cooking time: 45–50 minutes

Calories per serving: 390

Freezing: recommended

A pleasant change from meat lasagne, this recipe is slightly lighter and very flavoursome. Serve with a crisp, No Point salad.

low fat cooking spray

1 large onion, chopped

2 garlic cloves, crushed

2 courgettes, sliced

140 g (5 oz) frozen or canned sweetcorn, drained

400 g can of chopped tomatoes

200 g (7 oz) canned tuna in brine

50 g (1³⁄4 oz) low fat spread

3 tablespoons plain white flour

1 teaspoon mustard powder

450 ml (16 fl oz) skimmed milk

8 sheets of no pre cook lasagne

40 g (1¹⁄2 oz) grated half fat Cheddar cheese

salt and freshly ground black pepper

1 Spray a medium saucepan with low fat cooking spray and fry the onion and garlic for 4–5 minutes, until softened.

2 Add the sliced courgettes, sweetcorn and chopped tomatoes and cook, uncovered, for 15 minutes. Stir in the flaked tuna.

3 Preheat the oven to Gas Mark 6/ 200°C/fan oven 180°C.

4 Melt the low fat spread in a small saucepan. Add the flour and mustard powder. Stir well for 1 minute.

5 Gradually add the milk and whisk after every addition. Continue whisking until the sauce is thick and smooth. Season well.

6 Spoon one third of the tuna and courgette mixture into a shallow ovenproof baking dish and top with half the lasagne sheets. Spoon in another third of the tuna mixture and cover with the remaining lasagne sheets. Top with the remaining mixture.

7 Pour over the white sauce and top with the grated cheese.

8 Bake in the oven for 45–50 minutes, until the top is golden and bubbling.

Variation For a totally vegetarian option, omit the tuna and add 400 g (14 oz) canned kidney beans and use half fat vegetarian Cheddar cheese. The Points will increase to 7 per serving.

NUTTY CHICKPEA CRUMBLE

32 Points per recipe

Serves 6

Preparation time: 20 minutes

Cooking time: 15–20 minutes

Calories per serving: 325

Freezing: recommended for up to 1 month

A very substantial meal, to be enjoyed by all.

low fat cooking spray

1 onion, chopped

2 garlic cloves, crushed

1 celery stick, sliced

2 carrots, peeled and chopped

4 tomatoes, chopped

125 g (4¹⁄2 oz) baby sweetcorn, halved

50 g (1³⁄4 oz) red lentils

410 g can of chickpeas

300 ml (¹⁄2 pint) vegetable stock

salt and freshly ground black pepper

For the crumble

50 g (1³⁄4 oz) cashew nuts

60 g (2 oz) pecan nuts

100 g (3¹⁄2 oz) plain flour

60 g (2 oz) low fat spread

1 Spray a medium pan with low fat cooking spray and sauté the onion and garlic for 2–3 minutes.

2 Add the celery, carrots, tomatoes and baby corn. Stir well. Cook for 3–4 minutes.

3 Stir in the lentils and chickpeas then pour over the stock. Season and bring to a simmer and continue to simmer for 15 minutes.

4 Preheat the oven to Gas Mark 6/ 200°C/fan oven 180°C.

5 Meanwhile, place the nuts and flour in a food processor and blitz for a few seconds to chop up the nuts. Add the low fat spread and blitz until the mixture resembles chunky breadcrumbs.

6 Pour the chickpea and vegetable mixture into a baking dish and spoon over the crumble. Bake in the oven for 15–20 minutes until golden.

Variation If you have Points to spare, crumble 50 g (1³⁄4 oz) of Stilton and stir it into the topping before spooning it over the vegetables. The Points per serving will be 6¹⁄2.

**Tuna Lasagne:
Discover a tasty
new way to
enjoy lasagne
for 6 Points.**

Home Made Pizza: With pizza that tastes this good for only 6 Points, losing weight has never been more fun!

HOME MADE PIZZA

24½ Points per recipe

Ⓥ Serves 4

*Preparation and cooking time:
20 minutes + 1 hour 10 minutes–
1 hour 40 minutes standing
Calories per serving: 355
Freezing: not recommended*

Making your own pizzas is such good fun, especially if you have children to help you. They taste great and the best part is that they are so low in Points.

For the base

*200 g (7 oz) strong white flour plus
2 teaspoons for rolling
½ teaspoon salt
½ sachet dried yeast
low fat cooking spray*

For the topping

*400 g (14 oz) canned chopped tomatoes
300 g (10½ oz) frozen spinach,
defrosted and drained*

*2 tomatoes, sliced
2 spring onions, chopped
70 g (2½ oz) grated mozzarella
light cheese
150 g (5½ oz) grated half fat cheddar
salt and freshly ground black pepper*

1 Place the flour and salt in a large bowl. Make a well in the centre and add 125 ml (4½ fl oz) tepid water.

2 Sprinkle over the yeast and leave to stand for 5 minutes.

3 Stir the water to dissolve the yeast and gradually draw in the flour to make a soft dough.

4 Turn out the dough on to a floured surface and knead the dough until smooth.

5 Spray a clean bowl with low fat cooking spray. Cover and leave it to rise until doubled in size. This will take about 1–1½ hours.

6 Punch the dough to take out the air.

7 Shape the dough into a ball. Cover it with a cloth and leave to rest for 10 minutes.

8 Place the dough ball on a lightly

floured surface and roll to a 30 cm (12 inch) round. Place the dough on a baking sheet.

9 Preheat the oven to its hottest temperature and place the shelves near the top.

10 Spread the tomatoes over the dough, then top with the remaining ingredients, finishing with the cheeses. Spread the toppings evenly, leaving a small clean edge around the dough.

11 Bake in the oven for 8–10 minutes, until the base of the pizza is golden.

Top tip Try not to add too much flour when kneading and rolling, as this will make the dough tougher and not so light.

Variation For a different topping, use 400 g (14 oz) canned chopped tomatoes, 1 sliced courgette, 1 de-seeded and sliced red pepper, 90 g (3¼ oz) watercress, 100 g (3½ oz) drained, canned tuna in brine. Season to taste. The Points per pizza will be 5½ without cheese.

ASPARAGUS STUFFED PLAICE

11 Points per recipe

Serves 2

*Preparation time: 20 minutes
Cooking time: 30 minutes
Calories per serving: 370
Freezing: not recommended*

These stuffed plaice are very light but have a delicious rich, creamy sauce. They make an impressive and attractive meal to serve to family and friends.

*2 medium plaice fillets, cut in half lengthways
150 g (5½ oz) asparagus tips, trimmed
300 ml (10 fl oz) semi skimmed milk*

*1 teaspoon wholegrain mustard
2 teaspoons low fat spread
1 tablespoon plain white flour
40 g (1½ oz) grated Parmesan cheese
salt and freshly ground black pepper*

1 Preheat the oven to Gas Mark 6/ 200°C/fan oven 180°C.

2 Lay each of the four pieces of fillet on a board. Divide the asparagus tips between the fillets and place them at the end of each fish. Gently roll up the fillets, keeping the asparagus tips inside.

3 Place the rolls in a baking dish. Mix together the milk and the wholegrain mustard, and then pour this over the fillets. Season and place them in the oven for 30 minutes.

4 Remove the rolls from the oven and pour off the milk, reserving 150 ml (5 fl oz) of it.

5 Melt the low fat spread in a small saucepan and mix in the flour. Pour the reserved milk in the pan and bring to a simmer, stirring constantly until it starts to thicken.

6 Preheat the grill to high.

7 Pour the white sauce over the rolls and sprinkle over the grated Parmesan.

8 Grill the fish for 5–6 minutes or until golden. Serve immediately.

Variation For a real treat, stuff the plaice fillets with 100 g (3½ oz) prawns instead of asparagus – cooking for slightly less time. The Points per serving will then be 6½.

4 Cook in the oven for 30–35 minutes.

5 Spray a small saucepan with low fat cooking spray and gently sauté the shallot for 3–4 minutes.

6 Preheat the grill.

7 Remove the chops from the oven and pour off the liquid into the small pan with the shallot.

8 Place the chops under the grill to brown the potatoes.

9 Stir the crème fraîche into the shallot mixture. Check the seasoning. Serve the chops on two warmed plates drizzled with the sauce.

Top tip Cooking potatoes this way is so easy and really does look good – try it with other meat steaks or even fish, remembering to alter the Points accordingly.

Mustard Pork Chops: A family favourite for 6 Points.

MUSTARD PORK CHOPS

12½ Points per recipe

Serves 2

Preparation time: 20 minutes

Cooking time: 35 minutes

Calories per serving: 530

Freezing: not recommended

Make this dish when friends come round for supper; it is so easy to make, but looks really impressive. Serve with broccoli and mashed swede to mop up the juices.

2 medium pork loin chops

1 teaspoon wholegrain mustard

90 g (3¼ oz) potatoes, peeled

low fat cooking spray

1 shallot, diced

1 tablespoon half fat crème fraîche

salt and freshly ground black pepper

1 Preheat the oven to Gas Mark 4/ 180°C/fan oven 160°C.

2 Place the pork chops in a shallow ovenproof dish and spread the mustard over each one.

3 Thinly slice the potatoes and place them in a layer on top of the mustard covered chops, overlapping them so they resemble fish scales. Spray the potatoes with low fat cooking spray.

COCONUT SYRUP PUDDING

32 Points per recipe

 Serves 6

Preparation and cooking time:
15 minutes

Calories per serving: 290

Freezing: not recommended

Forget the four hours of steaming required – this pudding takes just minutes in the microwave but tastes as good as the real thing!

100 g (3½ oz) self raising white flour

30 g (1¼ oz) desiccated coconut

30g (1¼ oz) fruit sugar

100 g (3½ oz) low fat spread

2 eggs

4 tablespoons Golden Syrup

300 ml (10 fl oz) low fat custard, heated, to serve

1 Place the flour, coconut, fruit sugar, low fat spread, eggs and 1 tablespoon of the Golden Syrup in a food processor or electric mixer. Blend until mixed to a batter.

2 Place the remaining Golden Syrup in the base of a 1.2 litre (2 pint) pudding basin, and then spoon the cake mixture over the top.

3 Cover the pudding basin with clingfilm, piercing it a few times with a sharp knife.

4 Place the bowl in the microwave and cook on full power for 4 minutes.

5 Allow the pudding to stand for 2 minutes then turn it out on to a plate.

6 Serve the pudding cut into wedges with the hot custard.

Variation For a chocolate flavoured pudding, substitute 50 g (1¾ oz) of flour for cocoa powder, and instead of the coconut add 30 g (1¼ oz) chopped dates. The Points per serving will then be 4.

BAKED LIME CHEESECAKE

59½ Points per recipe

 Serves 10

Preparation time: 15 minutes

Cooking time: 1 hour 10 minutes + 2 hours cooling

Calories per serving: 275

Freezing: not recommended

A creamy, but sharp, thick topping and a crunchy ginger base make this the perfect baked cheesecake. Serve with fresh fruits if you have Points to spare.

low fat cooking spray

180 g (6¼ oz) gingernut biscuits, crushed

40 g (1½ oz) low fat spread, melted

300 g (10½ oz) Quark

200 g (7 oz) cream cheese

60 g (2 oz) fruit sugar (fructose)

4 large eggs

finely grated zest and juice of 4 limes, plus extra to decorate

1 Preheat the oven to Gas Mark 3/ 160°C/fan oven 140°C. Spray a 20 cm (8 inch) loose bottomed tin with low fat cooking spray.

2 Mix the crushed biscuits and melted low fat spread together and press the mixture into the base of the tin.

3 Bake in the oven for 10 minutes. Meanwhile, whisk together the Quark, cream cheese, fruit sugar and eggs until smooth.

4 Beat in the grated lime zest and juice.

5 Pour the cheese mixture over the baked biscuit base and return to the oven for 1 hour.

6 After 1 hour, turn off the oven and leave the cheesecake for another 2 hours before removing and chilling in the fridge (the top may crack but that is fine). Decorate with the lime zest.

Top tip The quickest way to crush the gingernut biscuits is in a food processor, but don't over process

them or you will have powder instead of nice chunky bits.

Variation Use lemons instead of limes if you wish. The Points will remain the same.

Baked Lime Cheesecake: Enjoy a slice for 6 Points.